MW01283818

The Campus History Series

UNIVERSITY OF
THE PACIFIC

The Campus History Series

UNIVERSITY OF THE PACIFIC

NICOLE GRADY MOUNTJOY
EDITED BY MIKE WURTZ AND LISA K. MARIETTA

ARCADIA
PUBLISHING

Published by Arcadia Publishing
Charleston, South Carolina

Printed in the United States of America

Library of Congress Control Number: 2021933340

For all general information, please contact Arcadia Publishing:
Telephone 843-853-2070
Fax 843-853-0044
E-mail sales@arcadiapublishing.com
For customer service and orders:
Toll-Free 1-888-313-2665

Visit us on the Internet at www.arcadiapublishing.com

To the past, current, and future Pacificans, who have and will make the University of the Pacific what it is

CONTENTS

ACKNOWLEDGMENTS

I would like to thank all the Pacificans who have carefully collected the history of University of the Pacific and therefore helped establish what would become the Holt-Atherton Special Collections and Archives, where that history is now preserved and shared. I am forever grateful to Mike Wurtz, head of special collections, and Mary Somerville, the university librarian, for giving me the opportunity to tackle this project. Thank you to my husband, Nicholas, who agreed to me taking over his man cave during the pandemic and was patient with my need to spend so many odd hours writing this book.

It is heartbreaking to create a book like this knowing there is no way to tell every rich story or include every person who contributed to University of Pacific's history. An attempt to do so would take, oh, 170 years! There are many more stories that "shoulda" been in here, and likewise, there may be a story or two included that someone will judge as unneeded—but try telling that to the people in the photographs. Readers who want to further explore the depth and breadth of this university's history will be happy to know that former provost Philip N. Gilbertson's 2016 book, *Pacific on the Rise: The Story of California's First University*, is available for free through Pacific's Scholarly Commons collection of online information. Lastly, we invite you to come and explore Pacific's history directly from the source in the University Archives. The staff is here to help you discover, or rediscover, your Pacific story.

Unless otherwise noted, all images used in this book come from the Holt-Atherton Special Collections and Archives or the Office of University Strategic Communications.

INTRODUCTION

Since its founding as California's first university in 1851, University of the Pacific has lived up to its commitment not only to its students, faculty, and staff, but also the communities in which it resides. Today, Pacific's mission is to provide a superior, student-centered learning experience integrating liberal arts and professional education and preparing individuals for lasting achievement and responsible leadership in their careers and communities. It is a mission built upon values such as academic excellence, community engagement, diversity and inclusion, integrity and accountability, and respect and civility. These collective ideals are achieved through the collaboration of the remarkable individuals who have invested in Pacific over the years.

Pacific has always been a trailblazer, and it continues to support innovative programs and to expand and grow both physically and academically. In addition to being California's first chartered university, Pacific was the first to offer coeducational learning, the first on the West Coast to have a music conservatory, the first to offer an undergraduate teacher corps program, the first to require all students in its international program to study abroad during their sophomore year, the first in the United States to establish a dedicated Spanish-language college, and the first to offer a four-year graduation guarantee. Today, Pacific's 10 schools and colleges offer nearly 100 majors and continue to build toward the vision of Pacific becoming the leading student-focused university in the nation.

There have also been struggles. Financial ups and downs as well as local, regional, national, and worldwide challenges have had an impact on the campus's programs as well as its overall mood and atmosphere, but Pacific has always risen to the occasion. In 2021, it was named one of the top 20 best universities in the West by the *Wall Street Journal/Times Higher Education*.

For much of its first 50 years, University of the Pacific was both a preparatory school and an institution of higher learning. A school of medicine was added in 1858, and Pacific expanded again when Napa College closed in the 1890s and all its students (including Pacific's first historian, Rockwell Hunt) became Pacificans. The physical campus also grew through the early years, first with a move from Santa Clara to the College Park neighborhood of San Jose in 1871 and then again in 1924 with the big move to Stockton.

Once Pacific was established in Stockton, the campus and programs continued to grow and change. By the 1950s, there was a School of Pharmacy, a Graduate School, and a School of Engineering. The 1960s saw an addition of three cluster colleges, which collectively evolved into the School of International Studies in the 1980s. This program became the first university-based undergraduate school of international studies in California.

In 1962, Pacific would extend its physical presence still further, this time to San Francisco with the acquisition of the College of Physicians and Surgeons, an independent dental school that later evolved into the Arthur A. Dugoni School of Dentistry. In 1966, Sacramento became home to Pacific's third campus with a merger with the McGeorge School of Law.

At the turn of the 21st century, Pacific was able to make vast improvements to all three campuses thanks to unprecedented and successful capital campaigns. Accelerated programs, experiential learning, and intense community outreach increased opportunities for students and cemented Pacific's presence and investment in Stockton, San Francisco, and Sacramento.

The University Archives, part of Pacific's Holt-Atherton Special Collections and Archives, are extensive. Staff curate over 1,000 feet of documents ranging from meeting minutes of the earliest board of trustees in the 1850s to the latest copies of the *Pacific Review* alumni magazine and other campus publications and student-generated content, such as the *Pacific Weekly* and the *Pacifican*, published online. The photograph collections cover every decade of Pacific's existence, and in recent years, the Office of University Strategic Communications (formerly the Office of Marketing and Communications and External Relations) has maintained a database containing photographs of students, faculty, and staff covering events in the 21st century. University Archives staff work frequently with students, alumni, faculty, emeriti, and administration to collect, preserve, and make Pacific's historical resources available for study and enjoyment. Thousands of resources are available through its website. More tangible artifacts, such as football helmets, school sweaters, and even a stained-glass window that used to hang at the College Park campus, can be seen in the Alex and Jeri Vereschagin Alumni House. Trophies and banners honoring successful teams and individuals can be found in the Pacific Intercollegiate Athletics Center and in other athletics facilities. Other objects of historical interest, including historic buildings, structures, and the two "spirit rocks," are scattered across campus, where they continue to instill the history and traditions of University of the Pacific.

One

THE SAN JOSE YEARS
1851–1923

University of the Pacific became California's first university under the name of California Wesleyan College in 1851. The following year, the board of trustees changed the name to University of the Pacific, having decided that "Wesleyan" was being overused by Methodist-founded schools across the country. Official discussions about creating an institution of higher learning in California had begun in 1850 among members of the Methodist Episcopal Church, including Bishop Beverly Waugh and the Reverends Isaac Owen, William Taylor, J.P. Durbin, and Edward Bannister. Pacific was first established in a modest building in downtown Santa Clara, in the San Francisco Bay Area, and preparatory department courses started in May 1852. There were four full-time instructors offering courses in English, Latin, Greek, French, Spanish, algebra, natural philosophy, and physiology. The first university class graduated in 1858 and consisted of five men and five women. A school of medicine was established in San Francisco in 1859 but was suspended between 1864 and 1869 due to low enrollment and the Civil War. Two other medical schools had opened by 1872, and Pacific's was reincorporated as Cooper Medical School in San Francisco, which eventually became the Department of Medicine at Stanford University.

Around 1866, Pacific bought a 435-acre parcel of land between Santa Clara and San Jose, called it College Park, and set aside 20 acres to build a new campus. The rest of the land was sold to cover debt and establish an endowment fund. Construction of the new campus began in 1870, and by 1871, the move from downtown Santa Clara to College Park was complete. In 1896, Napa College, a Methodist school in Napa, California, was absorbed into Pacific, a decision that was financially advantageous for both institutions, and in 1911, the board changed the name from University of the Pacific to College of the Pacific.

Rev. Isaac Owen arrived in California in 1849 as an appointed missionary by Bishop Beverly Waugh. As one of the founders of Pacific, Owen was assigned the task of acquiring the funds to open the university. He proposed the Santa Clara location and was on the first board of trustees.

Rev. Edward Bannister served two terms as president. From 1852 to 1854, he was the university's first president (called "principal" at that time), and he returned to the position in 1859, serving until 1867. Bannister came to California in 1850 with the intent of "establishing an institution for the higher Christian learning."

Rev. William Taylor, another founder of Pacific and member of the original board of trustees, was also a missionary assigned to California by Bishop Waugh, and he joined Owen in California in 1849. His home was used for the educational conference at which the decision of the location of the school was being considered.

Rev. Martin C. Briggs also served on the original board of trustees, and he was the first to officially hold the title of president from 1854 to 1856, following Bannister's term as principal. (Coincidently, Briggs had arrived in California on the same steamship as Bannister in 1850.) Between 1852 and 1919, Pacific had 17 different presidents and acting presidents, each one averaging less than five years of service. Starting in 1919, Pres. Tully C. Knoles began a new tradition of more long-term presidents, serving for 27 years.

Pacific's Female Collegiate Institute was completed in 1853, and "young ladies from a distance" were required to board there while attending school. Women students had been encouraged to enroll since the founding of the university in 1851, but they were educated separately from their male counterparts. The courses offered by the Female Department included bookkeeping, general history, physiology, botany, chemistry, logic, evidence of Christianity, and various high-level math courses, just to name a few. Embroidery and music were recommended if time permitted. This structure became known as the Kimberlinville Building after the university moved from Santa Clara to College Park in 1871. It was partially demolished in 1907 and then completely razed in 1931.

South Hall on the College Park campus was completed in 1874 and became the women's dormitory after the move from Santa Clara. Although the women roomed in South Hall, they attended class on the first two floors of East Hall, whose upper floors were used as the men's dormitory. Beginning in 1869, all students had the same teachers and the same classes (although not at the same time) and were, according to the catalog, "in all respects on a perfect equality with each other." By 1871, women and men were taking classes together, establishing coeducation in actual practice. When it ceased to be the women's dormitory, South Hall had various other uses until Pacific moved to Stockton in 1924, and the property was purchased for the Bellarmine College Preparatory high school, which remains there today. The building was likely torn down during the 1940s.

Tong Sing Kow (fourth row, second from left) was the first Chinese graduate of Pacific. Kow was a member of the Rhizomia Literary Society and graduated with a bachelor of philosophy degree on June 2, 1887. In the yearbook's "Diagnosis for the Senior Class," his character is listed as "original," his future profession as soldier, his hobby as "Ana-litics," and his favorite expression as "Say, boys." He was also a member of the Quaker group and the College Park Association of Friends.

Arthur Ki Satow (third from the left window, in front of the door frame) was the first Japanese student to graduate from Pacific. He was a member of the Rhizomia Literary Society and graduated with a bachelor of science degree on May 23, 1889. In that year's "Diagnosis of the Class of '89," he was described as an orator, artist, lawyer, statesman, and poet. After graduating from Pacific, he went on to attend the University of California's Hastings College of the Law.

Pictured is the south entrance of the Conservatory of Music, formally called the San Jose Conservatory and Chapel. Shown here in 1923, the building was constructed in 1890 and contained multiple instructional and practice rooms as well as the offices of Pacific's president and the dean of the conservatory. The ladies' literary societies Sophelectia and Emendia would hold their meetings in the building as well. The auditorium, which seated about 1,000, acted as a music venue, lecture hall, and chapel. The building was razed in 1938.

Pacific celebrated its first Arbor Day in 1895, with the university community coming together to clean up the campus and plant trees. It was an all-day event featuring manual labor in the morning followed by lunch and games in the afternoon. The tradition continued on campus in one form or another until the focus was shifted to Earth Day in 1970. In 1980, there was an attempt to renew the Arbor Day tradition, but it was unsuccessful.

Pacific's Department of Paleontology was home to both natural fossils and many casts of natural fossils created by the well-known American naturalist and professor Henry Augustus Ward of Rochester, New York. These items were displayed in a museum in West Hall along with other materials related to the natural sciences.

Music has always been a big part of Pacific's culture, even before the founding of the Conservatory of Music in 1878. This 1901 photograph shows Dean Pierre Douillet conducting the university choir. Concerts and recitals were and are still given frequently by students, faculty, and nonresident artists. According to the course catalog, "Only music of a high order will be rendered on these occasions."

In May 1901, Rome's original Temple of Vesta was reimagined as a float featuring Pacific students dressed as priestesses to recreate three famous paintings. The float was part of the Rose Carnival Parade held in honor of Pres. William McKinley's visit to San Jose during his tour through Northern California. The first Rose Carnival happened in 1896, and it became the Fiesta de Las Rosas in 1926.

The great San Francisco earthquake of April 18, 1906, shook the entire Bay Area, and the effect on Pacific's San Jose campus ranged from the "slight damage" to the observatory to the more substantial destruction of East Hall, which was "unconditionally condemned." The art room in the conservatory building had a hole ripped in the wall when its chimney detached during the earthquake. The report of the Buildings and Grounds Committee confirmed that all buildings needed repair—an unexpected cost and inconvenience that turned into a vastly improved environment for students and faculty. All buildings were repainted, some were refurnished, and the majority received either better heating systems or the promise of such in the near future.

East Hall was opened as the men's dormitory in 1885. In the years before its completion, the course catalog says male students were encouraged to "find board in private families convenient to the College, and away from the allurements of the City." In addition to living quarters on the top two floors, the building included lecture rooms, a museum, science laboratories, and space for the Young Men's Christian Association (YMCA) on the bottom two floors. The heavy damage East Hall sustained in the 1906 earthquake led to the removal of its fourth floor, chimney stacks, and ornate parapet. The building was razed in 1927, three years after Pacific had moved to Stockton.

As shown in this photograph from 1907, the stove-heated library gave students access to a full card catalog, plenty of current magazines and reviews, and the leading religious journals of the time.

On the College Park campus, the responsibility of ringing the university bell was an honor given to "trustworthy young men students" and "prominent preachers." The bell was also a popular target of pranks on April Fools' Day and other occasions, when students would carry on the tradition of taking the clapper out, rendering the bell useless to call students to class.

Since the university's founding in 1851 by the Methodist Episcopal Church, students have been required to attend chapel services regularly. This building was the main chapel of the College Park campus for the majority of the last quarter of the 1800s. The university sought to afford students "every possible help for development of Christian character" but stressed that it did not "emphasize denominational difference" or push a "particular form of religious faith, or in any way to discriminate against the adherents of any creed." Chapel attendance was mandatory until the late 1930s and was suspended by vote of the board of trustees in 1951 due to poor student turnout. The university's formal relationship with the Methodist Episcopal Church was severed in 1969; however, religious and spiritual life is still pursued by students at Pacific today.

In 1911, William Wealthy Howard (third row, far right) became the first African American man to graduate from Pacific. (The first African American woman, Mildred Elizabeth Jones, graduated in 1924.) Howard was a member of the Rhizomia Literary Society and graduated with a bachelor of arts degree. In the 1911 yearbook, Howard is listed as being "the only earthly thing that kept up their [the senior class's] reputation as a respectable crowd." He was also noted for his "strict attention to business" and for his role as "the presiding elder for the California Conference of Methodist Negro Churches." After graduating, Howard worked as a pastor at churches across the country and eventually received a bachelor of divinity degree from the Kimball School of Theology in Salem, Oregon, and a doctorate of divinity from Livingstone College in Salisbury, North Carolina.

In both the spring of 1918's Liberty Loan Parade (above) and the 1919 Homecoming Parade (below), students carried the College of the Pacific service flag. Each star represented one man from the university community who was serving in the Army or Navy during World War I, and the triangles represented those involved with the YMCA. Harriet Boss, who also built up the presence of the Red Cross on campus, had created the flag and marked the names of each serviceman in the individual stars. The two photographs show how much changed from one year to the next. By the end of the war, 314 Pacificans were in the service, and 3 had died.

When the United States joined World War I in late 1917, the Department of War asked young men between the ages of 18 and 21 to attend college as a form of military service and then enlist in the Student Army Training Corps. By the spring of 1918, forty-seven Pacific students had enlisted and almost 100 former students were already in service. Women on campus contributed to the war effort by organizing a Knitters Club to make socks, sweaters, and scarves for men in service.

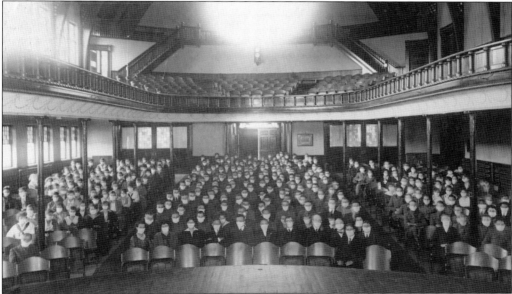

In 1918, an influenza pandemic swept around the world, but its impacts on the university were not well recorded. The student newspaper, the *Pacific Weekly*, did not publish any issues that fall, and when it returned in January 1919, it mentions only that the paper was returning to a regular publishing schedule again after an eight-month "leave of absence." The minutes from a board of regents meeting held around this time refer to the influenza as one cause of low enrollment and the change in quality of the students' work that term. This photograph from October 1918 shows that students, faculty, and staff on campus were taking precautions.

Tully C. Knoles was the 18th president of the university and had the longest tenure, at 27 years. He became president in 1919 after serving as head of the Department of History at the University of Southern California. Under Knoles's leadership, the university raised its educational standards and made the move from San Jose to Stockton in 1924.

Two

BEGINNINGS IN STOCKTON 1924–1960

By 1919, the College Park campus location was proving to be less than ideal, in part because of the proliferation of competing institutions in the Bay Area. Pacific looked throughout Northern California for a new location, and among the cities that made offers to host the university were Modesto, Stockton, and Sacramento—each one hoping to be the site of the first institution of higher learning in the Central Valley. Stockton won out for its central location and because it offered 40 acres and $600,000. In September 1923, students started attending classes in a building downtown, while construction began on the new site in April 1924. By September of that year, the Stockton campus was ready, and even more changes were in store.

In 1927, Pacific became an approved member of the Association of American Universities. In the 1930s, Pacific worked with local community members to create Stockton Junior College, and for nearly 20 years after that, all freshmen and sophomores at Pacific were technically students at Stockton College. The two schools shared the same campus until the junior college split off in 1951, and in the mid-1970s, Stockton Junior College moved about a mile up Pacific Avenue and renamed itself San Joaquin Delta College.

In June 1947, Pres. Robert Burns stated in his inauguration speech, titled "Pioneer or Perish," that "as far as Pacific is concerned, you can count on quality education as our goal. Not a 'small' college but a 'great' college. Not a 'bigger' college but a 'better' college. By seeking out the best faculty and personalizing our offerings, we conceive of a great work to do and one that has no visible terminus." Under Burns's leadership, many new programs were introduced, and Pacific experienced a time of notable academic growth that included the opening of the School of Pharmacy (in 1955), the Graduate School (1956), and the School of Engineering (1957). This growth would continue into the 1960s.

The 1923–1924 school year was a transitional time for Pacific. Most classes were still being conducted in San Jose, but many students began taking classes in Stockton at this downtown building on South American Street. The move created an immediate increase in enrollment among students in the Central Valley. Construction started on the Pacific Avenue campus in the spring of 1924, and classes started that fall. The entire issue of the *Stockton Record* of September 27, 1924, was dedicated to the campus's grand opening. For an entire week in March 1925, there were lectures, sporting events, and concerts to complement the dedication ceremonies for the completed buildings on campus.

This photograph from the mid-1920s shows members of the graduating class making their way to the auditorium in the new conservatory for commencement exercises. In the 1920s, commencement festivities were a weeklong event that included a banquet, a play, multiple addresses, a tea time, an Alumni Day, faculty programs, recitals, and finally, a commencement ceremony.

Located at the corner of Pacific Avenue and Stadium Drive, Manor Hall was built in 1924 to house women students not interested in housing on campus. Pacific purchased the building in 1932. Throughout the years, it has been used as a dormitory for women, for married couples, and for members of the Gamma Phi Beta sorority. It continued to be used as student housing until 2013. This photograph from the mid-1920s shows the sparse neighborhood surrounding Pacific's Stockton campus.

INFIRMARY · COLLEGE OF PACIFIC, STOCKTON. CALIFORNIA

West Memorial Hall was first dedicated in fall of 1926 as the West Memorial Infirmary. It was a gift of Harriot R. Jackson in memory of her father and mother, George and Ellen West, and of her brother, Frank Allen West. The building is now the Finance Center.

In December 1923, a delegation of Pacific students from the Foreign Students Club went to the 17th Annual Convention of the Cosmopolitan Club at Indiana University. The club's purpose was to foster understanding between foreign and American students to promote peace. By the 1924–1925 school year, the Foreign Students Club had separated into two individual clubs, the Chinese Club and the Japanese Club. These clubs helped to promote a better understanding of their respective cultures.

28

This aerial view of the Stockton campus in the 1920s shows just how remote the university may have felt in the early years. Today, Stockton and its neighborhoods surround Pacific, giving students the feeling that the school and the city are closely intertwined.

This grand entrance was dedicated in 1926 as the Harriet M. Smith Memorial Gate to honor the mother of J.C. Smith, who donated the 40 acres of land on which Pacific's Stockton campus was built. In 1963, the campus entrance was redesigned, and the gate was moved south. Between 1911 and 1961, the institution was called College of the Pacific.

The cornerstone of the new campus was the Conservatory of Music's concert hall, which also included classrooms. In 1924, when the building opened, nearly one out of three students at Pacific were enrolled in the Conservatory of Music, and by 1928, the school was a charter member of the National Association of Schools of Music. This photograph from January 1929 shows one of Stockton's rare snow days.

Coach Amos Alonzo Stagg, the "Grand Old Man of Football," came to Pacific in 1933, at the age of 70, after coaching for 40 years at the University of Chicago. He was Pacific's head football coach until 1946, when he moved to Pennsylvania to cocoach with his son at Susquehanna University. After six years, he returned to Stockton and served as the kicking coach of the junior college team until he retired at the age of 96. Over his long career, Stagg was a major contributor to the foundation of the game of football, and he was a charter member of the College Football Hall of Fame. This photograph shows some final words from coach at the 1938 away game at which Pacific beat Chicago 32-0.

In 1938, Wilhelmina Harbert, a professor of music education and the director of the Music Therapy Clinic, taught the first courses that would eventually lead to the development of the Music Therapy Program at Pacific. By 1946, students from Pacific were working with patients at the Stockton State Hospital, using music therapy to improve the patients' conditions. In 1948, Marc Jantzen, dean of the School of Education, brought together the Music Therapy Clinic with the Speech and Hearing Clinic, the Remedial Reading Clinic, and the Play Therapy and Client Centered Counseling Center on campus to benefit from a grant from the Rosenberg Foundation. In this photograph from April 26, 1959, the dean of the Conservatory of Music, J. Russell Bodley, is presenting Harbert with a slide projector in honor of her "remarkable career in the pioneering of music therapy." The program officially celebrated its 80th anniversary in 2020 and continues to do great service for the Stockton community.

In 1938, university president Tully C. Knoles said one of his objectives for the upcoming centennial was to construct a building on campus to be used only for religious services, in keeping with Pacific's Methodist beginnings. The cornerstone for the Morris Chapel and Christian Education Unit was placed in December 1941, and the building was dedicated in April 1942. The chapel was named after principal donor and member of the board of trustees Percy Morris and his wife, Lillie Morris. The rose window shown here is one of many of Morris Chapel's beautiful features. The different rosettes symbolize the life of Jesus Christ on Earth. Even with its Methodist beginnings, the word "interfaith" was, from the late 1950s, used in Morris Chapel promotional material, which also included listings of non-Christian services in Stockton. The position of the chaplain has evolved over time from simply chaplain to university chaplain to, in 2008, university multifaith chaplain. In October 2010, a room attached to the chapel was dedicated as "Sacred Space" and described as "a place for underrepresented religious groups on campus to pray and hold services." Across campus there are designated mediation and mindfulness areas.

Stockton Japanese Receive Orders to Evacuate

PACIFIC WEEKLY

Woodcarving of Amos Alonzo Stagg on Exhibit

Vol 36.   College of Pacific and Stockton Junior College, Stockton, Calif., Friday, May 8, 1942   No. 30

LOCAL JAPANESE GO

Keilty, Reid Chosen for 'Faustus'

June 5, 6 Dates for Presentation

With the coming of June fifth and sixth, Christopher Marlowe's Dr. Faustus will be presented to audiences in the College of Pacific outdoor theater.

PLOT

The plot has a strong beginning, climax and ending. The story runs somewhat in this way: An erstwhile doctor, Doctor Faustus by name, is the type of man who is on a constant quest for knowledge. So much does he desire the fruits of this heavenly tree of learning that he sells his soul to the devil who is in the person of Lucifer, for twenty-four years. The document is signed in the blood of Faustus.

In exchange for his soul Faustus requires the services of Mephistophilis for that twenty-four year period to help him on his knowledge quest.

MAGIC

Lucifer also gives Faustus the power of magic and to prove the strength of the gift, Lucifer calls in the seven deadly sins from his lower regions.

TO WORK WITH EVACUEES

Lecturing above to one of his classes is Dr. HAROLD JACOBY, economics and sociology professor. He is leaving campus early next week for government work in a Japanese evacuation camp.

Latest Army Exclusion Orders Affect Fifty-Three Students

Cities of Stockton, Sacramento to Be Evacuated This Week

Exclusion of Japanese from strategic zones of the Western Defense Command today reached the City of Stockton. Fifty-three College students are affected.

From 8 a.m. today until 5 p.m. tomorrow, approximately 1500 persons will report at the Civil Control Station for this area in the National Guard State Armory building, 1420 North California street.

STUDENTS TO LEAVE

Stockton students from the College of Pacific and Junior College affected by Exclusion Order No. 53 include the following:

C. O. P.—Virginia Inouye, Henry Inoae, Grayce Kaneda, Toshio Kaneda, Ida June Takagishi, Roy Teshima.

S. J. C.—Elsie Agari, George Akimoto, Sadao Baishiki, Frank Doi, James Doi, Richard Doi, Dick Fujii, Lillian Funisaki, Teruo Hirose, Tom Hoshiyama, Aster Iguchi, Fasae Inouya, Tokie Inouya, June Ishimaru, Yoshita Itaya, Shiziko, Fumi Iwata, Toshiko Iwata, Nobuko Kamatani, Kay Kaneda, Toshie Kaneda, Henry Kusama, Kinge Matsuhiro, Akira Mikasa, Kikuko Morita, Haruko Morita, Hiroshi Nishi, Warren Nitta, Arthur Noma, Keichi Ogasaware, Mary Oka-

MSS Sales Begin; Contest Winner to Be Announced

Interested students were signing their names on bulletin board lists last week, making sure that they would receive copies of MSS, student literary magazine.

Winners of the short-story contest will not be made known until the magazine goes on sale. However, it can be said that such student authors as Clint Sherwood, Ed Keilty, Merle Esplen, Margaret Stimmann and Ed Levin all have representative manuscripts in the publication.

The price of the magazine, purported to be the best in history, will be 35 cents. Considering the quality of the material contained in the publication it is allegedly

On February 19, 1942, Pres. Franklin D. Roosevelt authorized Executive Order 9066, which allowed the government to relocate all people of Japanese ancestry from some Western states to internment camps. This order affected more than 112,000 people on the West Coast, over half of whom were US citizens. Shown here is an article listing some of the more than 50 students who were forcibly removed from the Pacific and Stockton College campuses. Copies of this photograph were given to departing students at a dinner held for them by the Student Christian Association in April 1942. Most of these students would remain in the camps until after it was proclaimed on December 17, 1944, that internees could return home. At the 2013 commencement, seven internees were honored and given honorary degrees, six posthumously.

On March 16, 1943, fifty-eight Pacific men who were members of the US Army's Enlisted Reserve Corps were called to active duty. In the photograph above, classmates, parents, and professors gather to send them off. Most of the men probably ended up in officer training programs in colleges across the country. A few months later, Pacific itself became home to one of several V-12 Navy College Training Programs, and hundreds of men took part each term. The photograph below shows a group of trainees in front of Morris Chapel after services. The V-12 Program was active from July 1, 1943, through June 30, 1946, and many men in the program returned to Pacific after the war to continue their education. Over 2,000 Pacificans, both men and women, served in World War II, and an unknown number gave their lives for their country.

In 1944, Pacific purchased the Fallon House Theatre, located about an hour away in Columbia, California. The venue, like many other buildings in downtown Columbia, was constructed during the Gold Rush era of the late 1840s and early 1850s. When the Columbia State Historic Park was established in 1945, Pacific deeded the theater to the state. Starting in 1949, the Pacific Summer Repertory Company performed multiple plays there throughout the season, and students could earn college credit for their work. The program ended sometime before 1990 due to financial considerations. Shown here is director DeMarcus Brown (first row, fifth from right) with the theater company in 1965.

Pacific students have always been involved in the local community. The campus radio station covered local elections, and, as shown in this photograph from the mid-1940s, students helped tally votes during at least one election for Stockton's city council, school directors, police judges, and amendments.

In 1946, at the age of 37, Robert E. Burns (left) became the 19th president of Pacific, the youngest person to take the helm of a university in the West. Outgoing president Tully C. Knoles was named chancellor. Burns had enrolled as a student at Pacific in 1927, graduated in 1931, and since then had worked his way up through different administrative departments on campus. In 1941, he became assistant to the president, and five years later, Knoles (right) handed over the presidency.

Surplus Quonset huts began showing up on campus in 1946. Initially, one was used as a men's dormitory, another for the physics and geology departments, and another to house the campus FM radio station KCVN (later KUOP). According to the *Pacific Review*, the radio station hut included "studios, classrooms, transmitting and operating rooms, and offices." These structures were used for a variety of purposes and departments for more than half a century; by 2001, they had all been removed.

Prof. Lawton Harris's passion for international folk dance started well before he came to Stockton in 1942, and at Pacific, he continued to build his reputation for studying, performing, and teaching folk dance to many devoted followers. In 1948, he started the Folk Dance Camp, and he served as the camp director until his death in 1967. The camp grew to include multiple classes, parties, talent shows, people in costume, shopping opportunities, and auctions. It is the oldest folk dance camp on the West Coast and still attracts participants from around the world.

38

Elaine Brink Stanley created the compass rose that can be found between Knoles Hall and Burns Tower. She graduated from the art department in 1941 and designed and completed the mosaic in 1949 as part of her master's degree. The center of the mosaic is the official seal of Pacific, which is surrounded by sections marking the four cardinal directions and the four principal academic divisions of Pacific. According to the *Pacific Review*, "Fine arts are represented by the musical lyre and the mask of drama. The balances of justice represent the social sciences. Physical sciences are denoted by a microscope. Health and physical education symbols are the caduceus, a tennis racquet and a bat and ball."

This photograph shows Bannister Hall (right) and Owen Hall (left) after their dedications in 1948. Both buildings were remodeled barracks that had been used during World War II for Navy personnel at Camp Shoemaker in Dublin, California. They were named for University of the Pacific founders and have served multiple purposes throughout the years. In the beginning, they were used for classrooms, the campus radio station, and library study space. In the 1950s, Bannister Hall was used for speech clinics, and in the 1970s, Owen Hall was used for additional practice space for the Conservatory of Music.

Prof. Alden E. Noble started hosting "summer biological activities" at Dillon Beach in Marin County in 1933; it would later be called the Pacific Marine Station. The photograph shows Noble (third from left) and Marc Jantzen, dean of the School of Education (second from left), making a preliminary examination of specimens brought in from a field trip with students in 1947.

By 1948, construction was completed on the Pacific Marine Station (PMS), and by 1957, a year-round program was running under the directorship of Joel W. Hedgpeth. College and university students—from Pacific and elsewhere—went to PMS for biological research and to gain leadership skills in the natural sciences. Specimens collected at PMS were shared with the Smithsonian and other museums. The photograph, from the early 1960s, shows the extent of the specimens housed at PMS. The program was phased out starting in 1978.

The celebration of Pacific's centennial, titled "A Golden Century Crowns Pacific," was a yearlong event that included dedications, banquets, conferences, and guest speakers. Seen here are two students dressed in 1851 period garb at the bookstore participating in the activities.

In honor of the centennial, Gov. Earl Warren kicked off a nearly 50-mile relay race between Sacramento and Stockton, with 100 runners passing a torch at every half-mile on the journey. Lighting the centennial torch in Stockton on June 2, 1951, marked the beginning of the commencement week activities, which included concerts, senior class programs, the first annual Faculty Research Lecture and Banquet, Tully Cleon Knoles Day, alumni reunion events, and the commencement itself, pictured here.

This 1954 photograph, taken on the occasion of Rockwell D. Hunt's birthday, is endearingly titled "Three Giant Sequoias." From left to right are Hunt, director of the California History Foundation, who was named "Mr. California" in honor of his work in the state's history; the "Grand Old Man of Football," coach Amos Alonzo Stagg; and former Pacific president Tully C. Knoles, who is credited with having moved Pacific to its Stockton campus.

Pacific's School of Pharmacy was established in 1955 and was only the third pharmacy school in California at the time. Professional pharmacy groups in the Central Valley urged Pacific to create the school and helped acquire the funding to do so. The school started with a five-year program that included one year of pre-pharmacy studies and four years of professional pharmacy studies. The program included clinical pharmacy work, as seen in this 1961 photograph.

In the fall of 1955, registering freshmen were called upon to help transfer books from the old library to the new Irving Martin Library. By the end of the day, they had moved almost 10,000 books, but there were still over 25,000 books remaining. That year, the Pacific Student Association welcomed the largest incoming class to date, with over 260 freshmen.

The Irving Martin Library, named after the founder of the *Stockton Record*, was dedicated in May 1955. It was the first structure in Pacific's history to be constructed specifically as a library; all previous libraries, on both the San Jose and Stockton campuses, were only rooms in other buildings. Martin was not the only donor to make the library a reality, as more than 300 other people also contributed with donations of either money or books. The building was given a modern design with facilities that included a spacious lobby, a card catalog, a periodical reading room, book stacks, a reference desk, a reserve book room, a typing room, a microfilm room, a California room, workshop spaces, staff rooms, and offices. The second floor (pictured below) housed the main reading room, a circulation desk, a thesis room, 25 private study carrels, and more book stacks.

There is a long-standing story that says Southwest Hall was once a part of the Stockton State Hospital, but it is not true. South Hall (shown above) was built in 1924 as part of Pacific's new Stockton campus, and it was constructed specifically as a women's dormitory. In 1946, a new dormitory, called West Hall, was built immediately west of South Hall, and then in 1956, the two buildings were joined and called Southwest Hall (right). Perhaps part of the confusion came from the fact that the West Memorial Infirmary (which was named for the West family) was built in 1926 to care for students who got ill.

Pres. Robert E. Burns and dean of women Catherine Davis show off a drawing of the new women's dormitory. When it was constructed in 1957, the Women's Residence Hall became the largest building on campus and could house 400 students. In 1960, the building was renamed in honor of Grace A. Covell, a prominent Modesto businesswoman, civic leader, former member of Pacific's board of trustees, and sister-in-law to donor and regent Elbert Covell.

Practicing in the Outdoor Greek Theatre behind the conservatory is the 1957 A Cappella Choir. Under the leadership of director J. Russell Bodley, the choir was nationally famous and toured annually for requested engagements, including an Easter sunrise service at Yosemite National Park's Mirror Lake. Himself a Pacific alum, Bodley joined the faculty in 1923 after his graduation and was director of the choir from 1934 until his retirement in 1972. In 1955, he became the 10th dean of the Conservatory of Music, and he returned to full-time teaching in 1966.

Three

A THREE-CAMPUS UNIVERSITY 1961–1995

Over the next 30 years, Pacific continued to evolve. The name changed from College of the Pacific back to its original University of the Pacific in 1961, and the school expanded with the addition of two new campuses in 1962 (School of Dentistry in San Francisco) and 1966 (McGeorge School of Law in Sacramento). During this period, Pacific joined other institutions of higher learning in experimenting with the idea of "cluster colleges," or smaller divisions operating under the umbrella of the university. Raymond College, named after donors Walter and Kate Raymond, was the first of the cluster colleges. It opened in the fall of 1962 as a liberal arts college focused more on education and knowledge and less on training and skills. Its curriculum emphasized teaching using the seminar method, and it did not teach to specific careers. The students were challenged to work faster and better by completing courses in a trimester system and studying in depth.

In the fall of 1963, classes began at Covell College. Named after donor and regent Elbert Covell, this second cluster college had a Spanish-speaking program, where English was taught as a foreign language. At the time, it was the only bilingual four-year college in the United States. One of its goals was to develop inter-American studies that would contribute to greater understanding among the nations of North and South America. Latin American students were given the opportunity of a US education, and North American students received superior training in inter-American studies.

The third and final cluster college, established "beyond the Eucalyptus Curtain" (a reference to the line of eucalyptus trees that gave the feeling of a divided campus), opened in 1966. Named after donor Ferd Callison, Callison College required that students study abroad their second year in a non-Western country as a way of developing empathy for that country's people. Due to economic factors and low enrollment, the cluster colleges faded away by the mid-1980s, but before Raymond and Callison Colleges were closed, they spent two years as the combined Ray-Cal College. In 1979, the international program was absorbed into College of the Pacific, and it would eventually end up being the foundation of the School of International Studies. Covell would hold on a little longer, closing in 1986.

Stanley McCaffrey served as president for 15 years starting in 1971 after the unexpected death of President Burns. He expanded programs such as University College and increased the size of campus through the purchase of the former campus of Stockton College. During McCaffrey's time as president, the university also reorganized the School of Business and Public Administration and opened the School of International Studies.

The 1961 homecoming queen, Diane Brizzolara, along with Marion Knoles, unveiled the class of 1950's gift to the Pacific Student Association: a tiger statue, which was installed at the north end of the administration building, now called Knoles Hall. The plaque and tiger were dedicated to Pacific's late president and chancellor Tully C. Knoles. The tiger was stolen in 1994, and there have been no leads as to its whereabouts.

In July 1962, the independent College of Physicians and Surgeons became the School of Dentistry, Pacific's sixth professional school and its second campus, this one located in San Francisco. One of the first priorities was planning a new building, and after a period of fundraising and grants, construction began on the $8.9-million structure located on the corner of Sacramento and Webster Streets in San Francisco.

Dedicated in 1964, Burns Tower was created for the practical reason of lowering Pacific's water bill. It had a water tank on top (shown at right) and business and administrative offices below. The *Pacific Review* reports that the tower specifications include the following: "Walls average 8-inch thickness. Inside Tower measurement, 30 ft. sq. Tower height is 155 feet to top of parapet plus 91-foot FM radio antenna [shown being attached in the photograph below]. Basement floor is 14 feet below ground. Construction required 40,000 man-hours, the skills of 25 different building crafts, 200,000 pounds of reinforcing steel, 6,000,000 pounds of concrete." The tower was named after alum and former president Robert E. Burns.

Pictured here is the first graduating class of Elbert Covell College on June 6, 1965. From left to right are (first row) Benjamin Lacayo Manaiza, Gilberto Zuniga, Francisco Evelio Monsanto Perez, and Efrain Diaz; (second row) Rosinda Mejia Batres, Jose Gilberto Arita, and Elizabeth Ramos. With the exception of Perez, who returned to his home in the Dominican Republic, all the graduates returned to their native country of Honduras to become teachers.

Pres. Robert E. Burns is shown speaking at the School of Pharmacy ground-breaking event on October 30, 1966, during homecoming. Pacific purchased 41 acres of land on the other side of the Calaveras River, to the north of the original Stockton campus, for new buildings for the pharmacy school. The plans also included a Continuing Education Center and tennis courts. The Long family was a major contributor to the funding of the new facility, and in 2001, the School of Pharmacy and Health Sciences was renamed the Thomas J. Long School of Pharmacy and Health Sciences.

University of the Pacific expanded to a third campus when Sacramento's McGeorge College of Law, founded in 1924, officially became a part of Pacific on October 26, 1966. In the photograph above, Pres. Robert E. Burns (left) holds the new sign with Judge Gordon D. Schaber (center, McGeorge's dean from 1957 to 1991) and trustee Sherrill Halbert (right). As the law school's popularity grew through the 1970s, Pacific constructed a new 11,000-square-foot classroom building and a three-story student apartment complex (pictured below).

The physiology-pharmacology amphitheater laboratory in the late 1960s allowed students to watch demonstration lectures in person, and a closed-circuit television system also broadcast the lectures to other parts of the facility. This room was one of many located in the new Pharmacy Center on the northern edge of the Stockton campus. The main building consisted of four wings with laboratories, a library, offices, and a clinical pharmacy. The distinctive rotunda included lecture halls and the DeMarcus Brown Theatre, where plays and events took place. The preliminary concept design of the new pharmacy school shows plans for the main building and the rotunda.

The dedication for the new School of Dentistry building took place during the 116th Founders Day celebration in May 1967. John J. Tocchini, who was appointed dean in 1953, remained in that position through the unification with Pacific and the completion of the building. The College of Physicians and Surgeons was founded in 1896, and instruction started in 1897 in the leased Federation Building on Howard Street.

Wood Memorial Hall was the first expansion of the Irving Martin Library building in 1967. With the new addition, the library doubled in size and gained an elevator to help visitors navigate the three floors and basement. The second floor offered much-needed study space (shown), and the stairwell landings were designated as smoking areas.

The Wood Memorial Hall addition of the Irving Martin Library was named in memory of John Thornton Wood by his parents, Fern and Donald B. Wood. In addition to the Woods' donation, funding came through a federal grant from the US Department of Health, Education, and Welfare and a federal loan (shown on sign).

Callison College faculty members and students arrive in Calcutta (Kolkata) before traveling to Bangalore for their year abroad in the late 1960s or early 1970s. Every Callison student left Stockton during sophomore year to become immersed in academic and experiential learning in countries around the world, including Japan, Taiwan, and Mexico. Students returned from these international programs with a deeper understanding of the world and were better prepared for careers in public service, foreign affairs, and many other fields.

The Wendell Phillips Center for Intercultural Studies was built for the academic programs of the cluster colleges. This December 1967 aerial photograph shows what it looked like the year it was completed. Phillips, a native Californian, was an explorer, archeologist, and writer. According to the *Pacific Review*, he "transferred to Pacific a substantial share of his royalty interests in a new Arabian off-shore petroleum concession" as part of an agreement to name this building after him. Unfortunately, the "royalty interests" amounted to only about $71,000, not nearly enough to fund the project, but the agreement could not be broken. In this photograph, the first campus swimming pool, built in 1937, can be seen north of the Phillips Center.

Today, almost every person on campus has their own computer, whether a laptop, tablet, or smartphone. That was not always the case, of course, and it was not until 1968 that there was any mention of a computer on campus. In 1969, the new pharmacy buildings housed the campus's data processing equipment, and by the early 1970s, Pacific finally opened its first Computer Center—the only place on campus students would have had access to this technology. In 1975, when the now McCaffrey Center was remodeled, it included a designated space for a new Computer Center. The computer seen in these photographs is a Burroughs B6700 that had a memory capacity of 6MB.

Students from the 1990s are shown here on the Donald B. Wood Bridge, named for local businessman and regent Donald B. Wood. The 320-foot-long structure across the Calaveras River connects the northern and southern part of the Pacific campus. The bridge and the Cowell Student Health Center were dedicated together in March 1970.

This mature pepper tree was saved and moved before construction of the Cowell Student Health Center, which was dedicated in March 1970. It was named for the S.H. Cowell Foundation, whose grant made the building possible. The three-story structure included a student infirmary, a campus clinic, and X-ray rooms. At the dedication, it was presented with an Award of Excellence from the City of Stockton.

Pacific's Stockton campus has been the filming location for over a dozen films and television shows, including *All the King's Men* (1949), *High Time* (1960), *Raiders of the Lost Ark* (1981), *Dreamscape* (1984), *The Sure Thing* (1985), *Flubber* (1997), *Dead Man on Campus* (1998), and *Indiana Jones and the Kingdom of the Crystal Skull* (2008). The 1970 film *R.P.M.* (shown here) was shot almost entirely on campus, but most of the other movies include only a few short scenes; the two Indiana Jones movies, for instance, feature only seconds of the exterior of the Conservatory of Music.

In his 25th year as president, Robert E. Burns passed away due to heart failure in 1971. He had been diagnosed with bone cancer in 1969 but kept it a secret, and even after his diagnosis, he remained active and attended to all his duties until he was hospitalized. Burns and Pacific were synonymous during his presidency, and that interconnectedness carried on after his death, when his ashes were permanently interred in the tower that bears his name. In this photograph, Burns is shown standing in front of the tower after its completion in 1964.

Stanley E. McCaffrey became the 21st president of Pacific in December 1971. He came to the university with 25 years of experience in business, education, and government. He was an alum of the University of California at Berkeley and later served as vice president at Berkeley from 1956 to 1960, after which he became chief executive officer and president of the San Francisco Bay Area Council. He was also an assistant to Vice Pres. Richard Nixon. His devotion to service culminated with a one-year term as president of Rotary International.

In 1972, a live tiger named C.G. came to campus for the filming of Disney's *The World's Greatest Athlete*. He was not the first live tiger to visit the campus, however. In 1950, philanthropist Lowell Berry donated Tommy Tiger as part of the dedication of Pacific Memorial Stadium. Tommy lived in one of the Quonset huts and was trotted out for football games, rallies, and parades until 1952.

Dedicated in October 1973 on Sacramento's McGeorge School of Law campus, the Center for Legal Advocacy was considered the "Courtroom of the Future." It was at the time the only experimental courtroom facility in use for training trial attorneys and for testing certain innovations in courtroom procedures. In addition to regular classroom use and occasional use for actual trials, the courtroom was the "focal point for experiments in every facet of courtroom procedure, including court design, court security, use of television, and the training of police officers to more effectively perform their duties in court," as documented by the *Pacific Review*.

Pacific's first swimming pool was built in 1937. In 1972, it was replaced by the Chris Kjeldsen Memorial Swimming Pool, named after the man who served as Pacific's swimming coach for 27 years until his death in 1962. He was himself a former Pacific student and had played football under Coach Stagg in the 1930s. The pool has been used for various aquatic events, including scuba diving demonstrations and classes.

Students celebrate an anniversary of the grocery store around 1976. Now called the Grove, the grocery store opened in 1974 in the nearly completed building then known as the University Center. The building was renamed the Stanley E. McCaffrey University Center (the McCaffrey Center, for short) in 1987 on the occasion of President McCaffrey's retirement. The building was the first new structure completed during McCaffrey's administration.

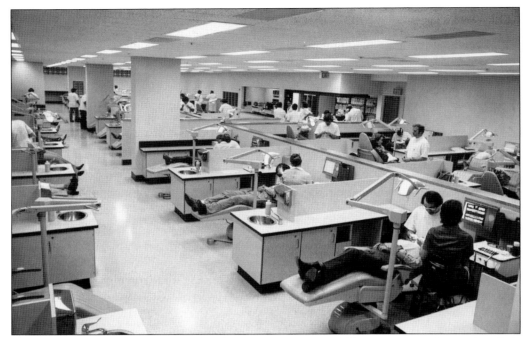

The School of Dentistry received a $700,000 grant in 1975 to renovate the main clinic (shown above) and teaching facilities in San Francisco. Besides the main clinic, the school had eight off-campus clinics that served the Northern California area, including the Union City location (below), which opened in November 1973 at a cost of $200,000. Before the Union City clinic opened, the area had only one private dentist serving an area population of 20,000 people. These clinics provided much-needed services to people who normally would not have access to them; in 1974, the nine clinics recorded more than 100,000 patient visits.

The *Pacific Weekly* was a half-hour television program that aired each Saturday on KOVR-TV (Channel 31 in Stockton) during the spring of 1976. Programming included news, sports, and special features on the university. The show did not return after the summer break. In this photograph, Howell Runion, an associate professor at Pacific's School of Pharmacy, exchanges notes before taping with Bill Keim, a graduate student in communication arts; Don Duns, chairman of Pacific's Department of Communication Arts; and Diana Clouse, director of the alumni-parent program.

When the cluster college program finally ended in 1979, students protested the closing of Ray-Cal. They staged a funeral march with two coffins, one representing Raymond College and the other Callison College, and the march ended with a formal eulogy at Morris Chapel.

The Holt-Atherton Special Collections and Archives (originally called the Pacific Center for Western Studies) was housed in the School of Education building (shown here in 1977) before it was moved in 1986 to the William Knox Holt Memorial Library. Special Collections preserves and provides access to the University Archives and one-of-a-kind manuscript collections such as the John Muir Papers, the Mayor George Moscone Collection, and collections on Japanese American internment, the Gold Rush, and other subjects focused on Western and California history.

From the summer of 1981 to the summer of 1982, Pacific's president, Stanley E. McCaffrey, took a temporary leave to serve as the president for Rotary International. During his tenure with Rotary, he and his wife, Beth McCaffrey, visited 70 countries and met with dignitaries all over the world, including Pope John Paul II. The Rotary Foundation supplied 10 scholarships to students from developing countries, giving them the opportunity to study one year abroad in the Pope's name. McCaffrey's theme as Rotary president was "World Understanding and Peace through Rotary."

Ground breaking for the Alex G. Spanos Center took place in August 1979, and after many delays, the $6.2-million complex was officially completed in September 1981. Above, President McCaffrey (left) and real estate developer Spanos (right) go over plans and designs for the 6,000-seat center, to be used for sporting events, university events, concerts, and lectures. The first series of community and university events to take place in the center was called Pacific Festival in the Spanos Center. Before the Spanos Center was built, basketball games took place in the Stockton Memorial Civic Auditorium, called "The Pit" by visiting teams because of its layout and lack of space. Below, the basketball team can be seen practicing in the excavated space of its new home.

Renovations to the newly named Faye Spanos Concert Hall were completed in 1987. Updates included replacing wooden seats with cushioned ones, redesigning the lobby, enlarging the bathrooms, installing central air and heat, and building an ornate glass-domed entry and box office. The renovations were made possible by funding from Faye's husband, local businessman Alex Spanos, and an anonymous donor. Pictured in front of the soon-to-be-renovated Conservatory of Music are, from left to right, dean of the conservatory Carl Nosse, Alex G. Spanos, Faye Spanos, and Pres. Stanley E. McCaffrey.

The William Knox Holt Memorial Library (above) was the second expansion of the original Martin Library. The library campaign began with pledges from the William Holt Foundation and from the late regent Holt Atherton, and the National Endowment for the Humanities also awarded a challenge grant to the university for the library's modernization. The addition increased shelving space as well as student study areas, from less than 300 seats to over 600. The library became the home of the Pacific Center for Western Studies, now called the Holt-Atherton Special Collections and Archives, which houses the University Archives and original manuscript collections. The funding goal of $6 million was tracked on a sign at the front of the library, as shown in the photograph below from the mid-1980s. The goal was reached and the building dedicated in 1986.

Built behind the Conservatory of Music in 1933, the Outdoor Greek Theatre hosted rallies and other student events. By the mid-1980s, the theater and all its wooden benches were completely removed and turned into a courtyard for two new buildings for the Conservatory of Music: the Recital Hall and the Rehearsal Hall. Both structures were funded by the same anonymous donor who helped fund the Faye Spanos Concert Hall renovation in 1987.

Four

LOOKING TO THE FUTURE
1995–PRESENT

Bill L. Atchley served as president of University of the Pacific for eight years, until 1995, when he was succeeded by Donald V. DeRosa. When DeRosa retired in 2009, he was replaced by Pamela A. Eibeck. Under DeRosa and Eibeck, the 24th and 25th presidents, the university enjoyed a period of growth that recalled the tenures of previous presidents Knoles, Burns, and McCaffrey.

President DeRosa "instigated a visionary initiative in social and emotional intelligence and brought strong leadership in whole-student learning and student life," according to the *Pacific Review*. While in office, he appointed Phil Gilbertson as Pacific's first provost, launched a matching Cal Grant program (the first in California), renamed the School of Dentistry and the School of Pharmacy after influential individuals, constructed two new residential halls and five other student-centered buildings, and expanded or renovated three existing structures. During this era, Pacific continued to be environmentally conscious, and in 2008, it constructed its first "green" building, eventually named the Don and Karen DeRosa University Center.

During her tenure, President Eibeck implemented "a bold vision to become a leading, student-centered university in Northern California." She pushed for more community involvement on all three campuses in hopes of establishing a stronger university presence in Sacramento, San Francisco, and Stockton. Eibeck kept Pacific competitive with peer institutions by modernizing the university's business practices, offering more competitive pay for employees, and creating a plan for long-term financial stability. The Leading with Purpose Campaign had achieved more than two-thirds of its funding goal before Eibeck's retirement in 2019.

The spring of 2020 was a game changer. When the COVID-19 virus caused mass shutdowns and quarantines around the world, people and institutions had to adjust. Pacificans shifted gears from the close, on-campus community that it is known for to a distance-learning paradigm that remained committed to giving students the quality of education and community they had come to expect from Pacific. It was under these conditions that the newest president, Christopher Callahan, took office in July 2020.

In 1995, Donald V. DeRosa became the 24th president of University of the Pacific—only the fifth since the campus moved to Stockton. During DeRosa's 14 years at Pacific, student enrollment increased, new construction and renovations boomed, and the Investing in Excellence Campaign reached its goal of $200 million a year ahead of schedule.

In 1997, the San Francisco 49ers football team signed a deal with Pacific to train its players at the Amos Alonzo Stagg Memorial Stadium for the next 10 years. Starting in the summer of 1998, the 49ers trained at Pacific, but after five years, the team broke the contract and decided to train instead at its facilities in Santa Clara. Pacific still collected the balance of the agreement.

In the early morning of November 18, 1995, a fire swept through Callison Dining Hall (above). An investigation concluded that arson was the cause, and a $6,000 reward was offered for information. There was a report that two people had been observed running from the scene that morning, but no one was ever charged. Due to the amount of damage (below), the building had to be demolished. Other structures affected included Elbert Covell Hall, which needed repairs due to smoke and water damage, and Raymond Great Hall, which required electrical rewiring. In total, the estimated damages were placed at $1 million. By 2000, the newly constructed Callison Hall was scheduled to open as a coffee shop/cyber café. Today, it is home to the Powell Scholars, recipients of the university's premier academic scholarship.

Judy Chambers served as vice president of student life for 25 years before stepping down in 2001. During her time in the position, she built a nationally recognized program and won many awards for her service at Pacific and in the community. Chambers started at Pacific as a student, graduating with a bachelor's degree in 1958 and then a master's degree in 1960 (under the name Judith McMillin). She came back in 1968 as an assistant to President Burns and eventually met her future husband, Dewey Chambers, who was a professor at Pacific. He taught in the education department for over 25 years, and during that time, he was a passionate advocate for children's literature and was himself the author of several books.

In 2001, the School of Pharmacy and Health Sciences was renamed the Thomas J. Long School of Pharmacy and Health Sciences in honor of the Long family's generosity to Pacific. The Longs Drugs chain was founded in 1938, and the Long Foundation has been a longtime supporter of Pacific, fully recognizing the role the university plays in pharmacy practice. Pictured here are, from left to right, pharmacist students Cory Ng, Beverly Pappas, and Yujie Yang.

In August 2004, the Arthur A. Dugoni School of Dentistry became the first dental school in the United States to be named after its current dean. Arthur Dugoni was a graduate of the school's forerunner, the College of Physicians and Surgeons, based in San Francisco, and he then worked as a professor at the school before becoming dean in 1978. He went on to become a national leader in dentistry and dental education. His career included serving as president of the California Dental Association, the American Dental Association, the American Dental Education Association, and the American Board of Orthodontics, and he garnered many awards. He stepped down as dean in 2006, but he remained involved with Pacific until his death in 2020 at the age of 95.

The American Institute of Architects (AIA) awarded Pacific's Baun Fitness Center an Award for Design Excellence in 2004. The building, named for regent, alum, and donor Ted Baun, was built in 1992, remodeled in 1998, and given its award-winning expansion in 2004. Amenities at the fitness center include free weights, various types of exercise equipment, a bike cycle studio, and a 36-foot-tall indoor rock-climbing tower.

The Don and Karen DeRosa University Center was completed in 2008. It was Pacific's first campus building to be certified under the LEED program. The 55,000-square-foot building houses the bookstore, cafeteria, a ballroom, meeting rooms, a restaurant called the River Room, and an open lobby for events. The DUC, as it is known, uses less energy and water than other buildings of its kind and includes a variety of other environmentally friendly features.

Pamela A. Eibeck became the 25th president of Pacific in 2009, and she is the only woman to have held the position so far. During her 10-year term, she continued the tradition of expanding and improving campus buildings and facilities. In a letter to the Pacific community, she emphasized the qualities that inspired her: "The hallmarks of a Pacific education—close faculty/student interactions; experiential learning; immersion in and giving back to communities; and preparation for a meaningful life—are what continue to equip our students to navigate the complexities of the 21st century."

His Last Tribute to Culture. A Christian Classical Education Will Never Be Regretted By Any One.

During a 2011 renovation of Baun Hall, a stained-glass window was found inside a wall that had been covered by a chalkboard, corkboard, and plywood. Research in the University Archives revealed that the window had once hung in the Conservatory of Music building on the San Jose campus. In 1938, long after Pacific had left San Jose, the building was being torn down, but the window was offered to the Stockton campus to adorn the structure being renovated to house the library. In 1954, the library moved across campus, and the old building eventually became the engineering department, named for alum and regent Ted Baun. This photograph from around 1900 indicates that there were two stained-glass windows. The window found in Baun Hall is now on display in the Alumni House; the fate of the other window remains unknown.

Dolores Huerta, cofounder of the organization that would become the United Farm Workers (UFW), received an honorary degree from Pacific in October 2010. She is seen here with Pres. Pamela Eibeck. After the ceremony, Huerta's official portrait was unveiled for display in the Architects of Peace collection, located in the Wendell Phillips Center.

Powell Scholars are described as "high-achieving students from across all majors who demonstrate leadership potential, pursue creative endeavors and innovative research, and become game-changers in their communities both locally and globally." The program was started in 2007 and made possible by regent Jeanette Powell and her late husband, former regent Robert C. Powell. The Powells also funded the renovation of Callison Hall so that the Powell Scholars would have a dedicated meeting space. Seen below are President Eibeck (left) and Jeanette Powell (center) at the Callison Hall dedication in January 2012.

Pacific's Beyond Our Gates initiative is "a community outreach effort focused on improving education and quality of life in Stockton and San Joaquin County." Beyond Our Gates promotes college attendance rates by having elementary and high school students visit campus for various programs as a way of increasing their interest in college. In support of the premise that those who can read proficiently by the end of third grade will have future academic success, Pacificans also visit various schools and have community family days on campus that include activities such as reading to or being read to by the university's mascot, Powercat; by people dressed as superheroes; by the current university president; or by visiting therapy dogs, shown here at the 2012 event.

The Biological Sciences Center is a 54,000-square-foot building with state-of-the-art technology, labs, and teaching spaces. Completed in 2008, the much-needed structure benefited the growing classes of science majors, and the labs provide space for groundbreaking research, such as figuring out a way to make black widow silk a renewable resource. Pictured is visiting assistant professor Kristin Kohler, one of the many people who was working in Prof. Craig Vierra's silk-spinning lab in 2013.

At the 2013 commencement, Pacific recognized the students of Japanese descent who had been forced into internment camps in 1942 because of Executive Order 9066 and never completed their schooling at Pacific. Former student Ida (Takagishi) Inouye (left) was there to accept her honorary degree in person from President Eibeck (right), and two other family groups accepted posthumous degrees on behalf of family members.

Virginia Chan and Tony Chan, both graduates of the Thomas J. Long School of Pharmacy and Health Sciences, met each other in line at their 1977 commencement and later got married. The Chans and their family, many of whom are also alumni, have left a lasting legacy at Pacific. In October 2014, that legacy was celebrated with the renaming of the renovated Brookside Hall to the Chan Family Hall. The Chans also funded the expansion of the Chan Family Health Sciences Learning Center (dedicated in 2008), the modernization of various classrooms, the establishment of several endowed scholarships, and the creation of a Student Success Center. From left to right are Jonathan Chan, Virginia (Chang) Chan, Megan Chan, and Tony Chan.

The Arthur A. Dugoni School of Dentistry's newest San Francisco home was dedicated on March 7, 2014. The seven-story, 395,000-square-foot campus was acquired in 2011 for $47 million. After two years of extensive renovation, the building is a certified LEED Gold Standard and contains teaching and patient-care facilities, classrooms, meeting rooms, and a simulation lab. The upper floors of the building are leased out for office space, but otherwise the building is home to not just the dentistry program but also the music therapy and audiology programs.

Ground breaking for the $1.5-million, 2,861-square-foot Janssen-Lagorio Performance Center took place in December 2016. The center provides state-of-the-art equipment for the conditioning and training of student athletes. Donors Kathleen Lagorio Janssen (a regent) and Dean J. Janssen are prominent Central Valley philanthropists and business leaders. Pictured are, from left to right, Bradley Davis, Damon Stoudamire, Pres. Pamela A. Eibeck, Kathleen Lagorio Janssen, Dean J. Janssen, Greg Gibbons, and T.J. Wallace.

Media X, a program within Pacific's Department of Art, Media, Performance, and Design, offers students a myriad of opportunities, such as collaborating with small businesses to create logos, websites, commercials, and marketing plans. Students can also work in the areas of theater, film, digital media, museums, content engineering, and sound engineering. The name Media X was reportedly first used as a placeholder for a final name, but the moniker proved to be appealing and has become permanent. Media X department chair Kevin Pontuti (left) and university librarian Mary Somerville (right) are pictured in the new experimental exhibition space located in the William Knox Holt Memorial Library.

In 2018, Pacific partnered with the Little Manila Foundation and the Filipino American National Historical Society Museum to recreate, albeit digitally, Stockton's famed Little Manila. In the early half of the 20th century, Stockton was home to the largest community of Filipinos outside of the Philippines, but in the 1970s, the neighborhood was almost completely razed in order to build the Crosstown Freeway. "Little Manila Recreated" allows virtual visitors to see the vibrant heart of Little Manila as it once was.

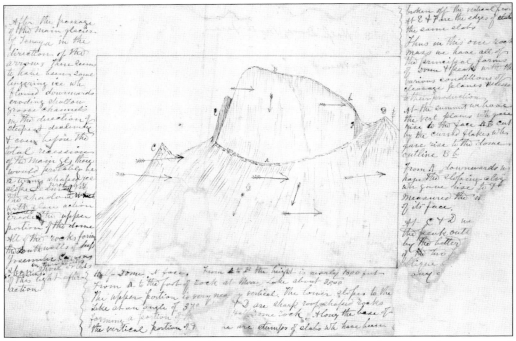

The spring 2019 issue of the *Pacific Review* shared the news that the university was proud to celebrate "the permanent gift of the John Muir papers and collection by the Muir-Hanna Trust." Described as "the world's largest collection . . . of Muir papers, journals, books and other memorabilia," the collection had been held on loan by the university since 1970 and housed in the library's Holt-Atherton Special Collections and Archives but would now be owned and "preserved permanently at Pacific, where it will be accessible to students, the public and researchers worldwide." This would also lead to the dedication of the Pamela Eibeck and Bill Jeffrey Muir Grove later that fall. (Above, courtesy of the John Muir Papers © 1984 Muir-Hanna Trust.)

In thanks to the generosity of a retired Stockton teacher, the School of Education was renamed the Gladys L. Benerd School of Education in 1992. Benerd's funding not only benefited the School of Education but also created scholarships and a library fund. Benerd was an alum of the Graduate School and School of Education and then became a health instructor at Stockton College during the time it was connected with Pacific. In 2019, the Gladys L. Benerd School of Education was combined with University College, Pacific's home for professional and continuing education, to create Benerd College, a "unit designed to take advantage of synergies and encourage innovation in program development and provision."

Juniors and seniors were able to move into the new Calaveras Hall in the fall of 2019. Among those pictured here with shovels at the ground breaking in September 2016 are regent Kathleen Lagorio Janssen, Pres. Pamela Eibeck, and Vice Pres. of Student Life Patrick Day. The two apartment-style four-story structures, built as the first phase in revitalizing student housing, include a recreational pool, an exercise room, a firepit, a community kitchen, and study spaces.

The 26th and newest president of Pacific is Christopher Callahan. Callahan had an interesting start, as he entered the position during the period when COVID-19 had basically shut down campus. Pacific is expected to formally inaugurate Callahan as president in the fall of 2021. Callahan has nevertheless worked with other administrators to safely navigate these trying times and lead Pacific through a successful period of distance learning.

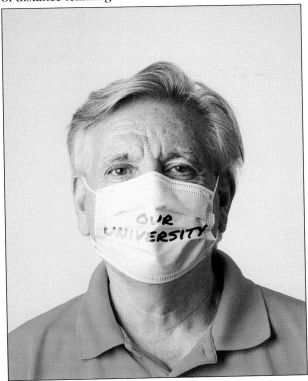

Pacific partnered with San Joaquin County Public Health Services to administer COVID-19 vaccinations starting in January 2021. Pacific's first delivery of vaccinations were specifically for Pacificans on the Stockton campus, including health care program faculty and students, health center staff, public safety personnel, and employees age 65 and older.

Five

STUDENT LIFE
PEOPLE, TRADITIONS, AND ACTIVITIES

The heart of any university is its students, and this is especially true at Pacific. Most of the traditions and activities on campus have come about because of the investment and involvement of the students themselves, and even through moving to a new campus and expanding to additional ones, the sense of community that Pacific instills has remained central to the university's identity. Of course, as times change, students change, and the importance of certain traditions often transforms with them. Sometimes the change is beyond their control, but other times they are the drivers of change when it is clear a tradition is no longer appropriate, inclusive, and/or practical for the university to continue.

These days, certain events that used to be part of Pacific life, like weeklong commencement exercises and homecoming programs, are no longer practiced. Traditions that started in the 19th century—for instance, requiring freshmen to wear dinks (a special kind of cap) or reserving certain benches for seniors only—eventually became outdated or just faded away. Traditions that focused on one particular group of people to the exclusion of others have either disappeared or been replaced with new, more inclusive traditions. Initially, students strolled the campus caroling at Christmastime, and later, Pacific presented the Festival of Lights. Most recently, students have been celebrating with the Holiday ROAR event, which focuses on community involvement.

Traditions have come, changed, and sometimes gone, but the feeling of community on campus has not. Pacificans take not only their education with them when they graduate but also years of memories and experiences, all of which contributes to their success as they go out into the world.

While traveling from Illinois to California in 1851, Olive Oatman and her family were attacked by a group of Native Americans. Olive and her sister, ages 14 and 7, were taken prisoner and eventually traded to the Mohave, with whom she lived for four years until she was returned to authorities at Fort Yuma. Her sister had passed away in captivity. Royalties from a book about the events, cowritten with pastor Royal Stratton, paid for Olive and her brother (who had been left for dead in the attack) to attend Pacific. This tintype shows Olive in 1857, the same year she attended the Female Collegiate Institute at Pacific. (Courtesy of Beinecke Rare Book and Manuscript Library, Yale University.)

Sanji Muto (to the right of the doorway leaning on column) came to Pacific in 1885 from Japan because his father wanted him to benefit from a Western education. He spent one year at Pacific before getting a job in San Francisco at the company that would later become the Kikkoman Corporation, famous for its soy sauce. When he returned to Japan, Muto worked for the Kanebo silk-spinning mill as a troubleshooter brought in to help save the failing company, and he soon led the company himself. Under Muto's leadership, Kanebo became one of the largest and most successful textile firms in Japan. In 1919, he established a fund at Pacific's library to support relations between the United States and Japan.

Pacific's first Death Valley expedition took place in 1937. According to the 1950 program, the tour of the Death Valley and Mojave Desert regions was "planned primarily as a scientific and educational trip, for studying nature in the rough." Students and faculty would start the 1,300-mile-long trip right from campus and camp out every night for nearly a week. The itinerary included points of interest such as Walker Pass; American Potash and Chemical Corporation in Trona; Ubehebe Crater; the ghost town of Rhyolite, Nevada; and many more geologic and historic sites along the way. Red Rock Canyon was a favorite spot to stop for a photograph of the whole caravan. Prof. Kurtis Burmeister's geology of California class's annual field trip studied "in the rough" in 2017. (Both, courtesy Kurtis Burmeister.)

Bob Bastian, a nationally syndicated editorial cartoonist who worked for the *San Francisco Chronicle* during the 1950s and 1960s, graduated from Pacific in 1940. Following graduation, Bastian studied art with Dong Kingman at the San Francisco Art Institute until the outbreak of World War II. A collection of Bastian's original drawings is housed at Pacific's Holt-Atherton Special Collections and Archives.

Golden Globe–winning actor Janet Leigh attended Pacific in 1943, when her name was still Jeanette Morrison. She studied what would become music therapy and was a member of the Alpha Theta Tau sorority, living on campus in the sorority house that now belongs to Kappa Alpha Theta. Leigh went to Hollywood before graduating but returned to Pacific and Stockton many times throughout the years, including when she accepted her honorary doctorate in 2004. Leigh's daughter Jamie Lee Curtis attended Pacific for one semester before following in her mother's footsteps toward a career in Hollywood. Leigh is joined by Pacific alumni actor Darren McGavin '48 and United Nations representative Richard Pedersen '46 on CBS's *Alumni Fun* on January 5, 1964.

Popularly known as "Mr. California," Rockwell D. Hunt, author of *History of the College of Pacific 1851–1951* and alum of Napa College, was responsible for having "Senior Rock" transported from Napa to the Stockton campus in 1951. The rock was originally a gift to Napa College from its class of 1893 (below). The initials on the side stand for Fay Donaldson, Iva E. Simpson, Lydia Ann Stuart, Leo C. Tuck, and Everett M. Hill. Napa College merged with Pacific in 1896. Students began painting Senior Rock in the mid- to late 1960s. In 2018, the team who was considering restoring the rock drilled a hole in the surface to assess the situation and discovered the paint was layered almost two inches thick!

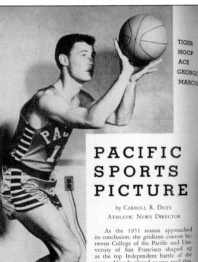

TIGER
HOOP
ACE
GEORGE
MASCONE

PACIFIC SPORTS PICTURE

by CARROLL R. DOTY
ATHLETIC NEWS DIRECTOR

As the 1951 season approached its conclusion, the gridiron contest between College of the Pacific and University of San Francisco shaped up as the top Independent battle of the year. Already played as you read this, the winner of the COP-USF game is the undisputed champion of the Far Western Independent teams.

The Tigers in 1951 were perhaps as good a football team as has ever represented the college. Fast, hard-driving backs, a large and mobile line both on offense and defense and a

This photograph from the 1950s shows a performance of the Annual Oratorio, held in the Civic Auditorium. The tradition was started by the Pacific chorus in the mid-1910s, and over the years, it grew with the Stockton community. The program was usually Handel's *Messiah*, and alumni would be invited to participate, along with various orchestras and choruses from the community. The annual event eventually tapered off.

George Moscone graduated from Pacific in 1953, having been admitted on a basketball scholarship. He was quite popular and served in various leadership capacities, including as president of the Rhizomia fraternity. After Pacific, Moscone earned a law degree and practiced law before starting a career in politics. He served on the San Francisco Board of Supervisors (1963–1966), moved up to the California State Senate (1967–1976), and was elected mayor of San Francisco in 1976, during a time when the city's political leadership began to more accurately reflect the diversity of the city's residents. In the fall of 1978, Moscone and supervisor Harvey Milk, the first openly gay elected official in the state's history, were assassinated by former supervisor Dan White.

Archite Teeterers Totter To Fame

Archanian fraternity members Steve Henry and Mike Resso shake hands after completing a 110-hour teeter-totter marathon in 1957 (above). The Alpha Kappa Phi juniors broke the 100-hour world record previously held by Archanians Duane Weaver and Jim Lane in 1951 (below). The teeter-totterers seesawed continuously, even while eating and sleeping, except for one five-minute break every two hours, which they had to take separately. *The Pacific Weekly* calculated that Henry and Resso traveled 157 vertical miles and registered "some 80,000 or more teeters, or totters." The event was picked up by local news channels and was featured in an article in *Life* magazine. In 1984 and then again through the 2000s, the spectacle became an annual event at which Archanians would teeter-totter for 72 hours in order to raise money for local charities.

Pictured here is the first commencement ceremony that took place at Pacific Memorial Stadium (later renamed the Amos Alonzo Stagg Memorial Stadium) in June 1961. The procession began with graduates entering under the scoreboard. Between 1932 and 1961, commencement ceremonies had taken place at Baxter Stadium, which was dedicated in 1929 and named after donor and board of trustees president Thomas F. Baxter. Prior to 1932, ceremonies took place in the auditorium or chapel. Starting in the late 1980s, commencement exercises were held on Knoles Lawn; in 2006, they moved to the Spanos Center.

According to the *Pacific Review*, Engineers' Rock was first brought to campus in 1962 by seniors Tom Decker, Al-Saleh Fawzi, Faisal Sultan Essa, Ken Kjeldsen, and Dave Dutra. The rock was placed in front of Baun Hall, which at that time housed the engineering department. In the 1980s, the rock was removed from Baun Hall because of vandalism, and three years later, it was installed in front of Khoury Hall, the new engineering building.

From the late 1950s to the late 1990s, the lawns on campus were flooded as a means of watering them. Each year during the peak of Stockton's summer heat, students gathered to body slide and lawn surf, as seen in this photograph from 1962. As shown in the photograph below from the mid-1950s, students could also take a few quick moments to cool their feet between classes. By the 2000s, water conservation efforts and the addition of underground sprinklers put an end to this summer activity. (Above, courtesy of Bank of Stockton Archives.)

The Pacific Music Camp for high school students, launched in 1946 by David Lawson from the Interlochen Music Institute in Michigan, brought world-renowned music conductors as visiting teachers and guest artists. Jester Hairston (right), who wrote the famed gospel song "Amen," was a frequent teacher at the band camp and received an honorary degree in music from Pacific in 1964.

The Band Frolic event began in 1929 as a fundraiser for the Pacific band. In between the band's performances, individual students and groups would perform vaudeville acts, competing against each other to be the best. Shown is a group from 1964. As this tradition continued through the years, the band performances were gradually dropped, and the show largely featured sororities, fraternities, and other campus organizations putting on a musical show, usually in drag. In the mid-1990s, the event morphed into a lip-synch contest that is still a popular part of homecoming festivities.

The columns between Knoles Hall and the William Knox Holt Memorial Library have a history going back further than their installation on campus. They were first erected in the 1890s as part of the Hazelton Free Public Library on Market and Hunter Streets in Stockton (above). In 1965, before that building was demolished, the city council voted to give the columns to Pacific. By 1967, the columns were reassembled as they are seen today (below). They were installed at a tilt in order that they would appear straight, as setting them exactly perpendicular to the ground would have created the illusion that they were bowing outward. The tilt is so slight that if an imaginary line were traced upward though each column, the lines would not connect until they were about one mile above the earth. The columns stand as a memorial to Grace Condit Weeks, Lois Condit Keys, and Ida Elizabeth Condit—the mother and aunts of Grace Burns, the wife of President Burns. Besides being an attractive and unique feature, the columns have a secret: if a person stands on the metal plate in the center of the rotunda and talks in the direction of one of the columns, their voice will be echoed back to them. The Stockton College class of 1951 dedicated a plaque for the columns in 2015.

Pacific's history of celebrating homecoming with parades goes all the way back to the 1920s. Throughout the years, student groups have competed for best float, many of which were designed around the theme of defeating the rival San Jose State Spartans or whichever team was slated to play against Pacific that year. The parade typically extends from campus down Pacific Avenue to the Miracle Mile. Early on, the floats were very elaborate (as can been seen by these in the 1960s), but in later years, the parades have increasingly been dominated by the marching band, cheerleaders, and the homecoming court.

The annual Strawberry Breakfast, first sponsored by the Young Women's Christian Association (YWCA), was started in the early 1930s and continued throughout the years, even as the YWCA underwent various changes. Today, the Center for Community Involvement continues the tradition of volunteerism that has for more than 100 years been carried out on campus by groups under the names YWCA, YMCA, the Student Christian Association, and the Anderson Y Center. The Anderson Y Center, which originally was housed in Anderson Hall, moved to its current location across Pacific Avenue in 1991. In 2004, the Anderson Y was renamed the Center for Community Involvement and built its reputation on tutoring and other community-based activities.

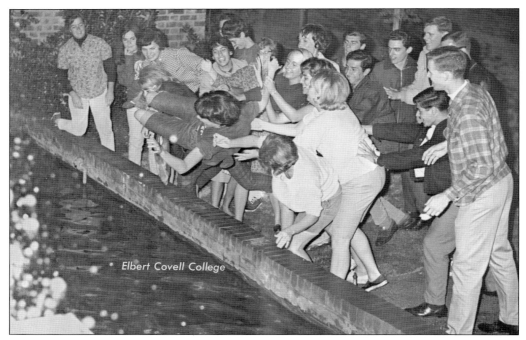

Elbert Covell College

Covelianos (as students of Elbert Covell College were known) socialized at El Centro, the student union, enjoying camaraderie, discussions of current events, study, rousing games of table tennis, music, Latin dancing, and dining, including at the Cenas de Gala formal dinner parties. In *convivencia*, Covell students relished intense talk with faculty and peers from different countries and ideologies. They also, on occasion, were known for throwing fellow students in the fountain.

When Pacific changed its name from College of the Pacific to University of the Pacific, Pres. Robert E. Burns commissioned internationally known London silver designer Stuart Devlin to design and construct the first academic mace for the university. The mace's first appearance was at Founders' Day ceremonies on March 6, 1966. Made of silver with gold plating, the mace is approximately four feet long and weighs approximately 15 pounds. It was a gift to the university by regent Winifred Raney. The mace is displayed at all official university functions, as it was at the 1969 commencement pictured here.

Let Us Vote (LUV), a national student campaign to lower the voting age to 18 and to "reestablish the identity of the American college student as a constructive, positive segment of society," was headquartered at University of the Pacific. Dennis Warren, a junior at the time, was the executive committee chairman and national chairman of LUV, and he formally kicked off the campaign by appearing on ABC's *Joey Bishop Show* in December 1968. The *Joey Bishop Show* broadcast nationally from the Stockton Civic Auditorium on January 11 (pictured), and by January 1969, LUV had established headquarters at more than 150 colleges, with over 1.5 million students enrolled. Musical duo Tommy Boyce and Bobby Hart even composed a song for the organization called "L.U.V." (back of album cover below). In part because of the efforts of the LUV campaign, on June 22, 1970, Pres. Richard Nixon signed an extension of the Voting Rights Act of 1965 and changed the voting age to 18 for all federal, state, and local elections.

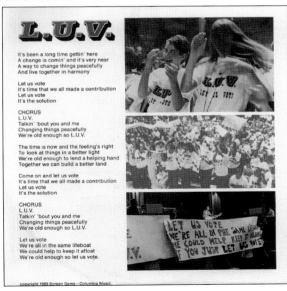

Pacific marching bands perform at various events, including rallies, parades, and halftime shows. The first evidence of a marching band at Pacific is the handful of musicians who played in 1901. The marching band had a cameo in the 1960 Bing Crosby film *High Time*, which was filmed on campus, and in 1969 and 1970, it was chosen to perform at the televised halftime show for the Oakland Raiders. With 110 members in 1970, it was the largest marching band in Pacific's history up to that point.

In the spring of 1969, a group of students protesting for change marched on Burns Tower, led by the newly established Black Student Union and MEChA (Movimiento Estudiantil Chicano de Aztlán). After listening to these organizations' demands and meeting with the Academic Council and other committees, President Burns started the Community Involvement Program (CIP), the main goal of which was, according to a *Pacific Review* report from 1969, establishing "200 full-tuition scholarships for culturally disadvantaged students." CIP is still going strong today.

Joining hundreds of thousands of others nationwide, students at Pacific participated in the Moratorium to End the War in Vietnam in the fall of 1969. Approximately 500 students took part in peaceful demonstrations on campus, one of which included marching with a flag-draped coffin. Some faculty canceled classes to allow their students to participate.

105

Here, Pres. José Figueres Ferrer of the Republic of Costa Rica meets with students from Elbert Covell College in the fall of 1970. Costa Rica's capital city of San José was the second location opened to students participating in the university's study abroad program. Students took courses at the University of Costa Rica, worked various part-time jobs in the area, and were hosted by local families.

Pictured here is the 1971 Black Student Union (BSU). In October 1974, the student newspaper quoted BSU president Vincent Lewis as saying, "One of the goals of the . . . BSU is to get involved in every aspect of UOP politics to help bring about decision making power with the administration." Established in 1969, the BSU continues to be an active organization on campus.

Pacific's community of scholars engaged in serious study against a backdrop of the 1960s and 1970s civil rights movement, sexual revolution, and anti–Vietnam War sentiment. The High Table dinners hosted by Pacific's Raymond College brought to campus distinguished guests from a diversity of disciplines, including poet Allen Ginsberg, Black Panther leader Huey Newton, the head of the right-wing John Birch Society, and activist Angela Davis. In a 1974 speech at Pacific, Davis said, "I know how these campuses mess with your mind."

In the spring of 1975, Pacific's civil engineering students launched their cement canoe, named the *White Fish*, in preparation for the first annual Cement Canoe Contest in California, sponsored by the student chapters of the American Society of Civil Engineers. The following year, Pacific's team took third place with the *White Fish II*.

Renowned jazz pianist Dave Brubeck originally planned to go into veterinary medicine before changing his major while at Pacific and joining the Conservatory of Music. Brubeck graduated in 1942 and then joined the military. Iola (Whitlock) Brubeck graduated a few years after her husband in 1945 and returned in 2000 to receive an honorary doctorate in law (shown at left with her husband and President DeRosa). Dave Brubeck had himself received an honorary doctorate from Pacific; his was in 1961 and for music. A plaque hangs in the Faye Spanos Concert Hall, where Dave and Iola first met in 1941.

Singer, songwriter, and actor Chris Isaak is a Stockton native and a graduate of Stagg High School. While at Pacific, he was part of the Community Involvement Program, and in 1980, he graduated with a double major in English and communication. Isaak is a Grammy-nominated singer and has released more than a dozen albums to date.

St. Patrick's Day was the first known occasion on which the "spirit rock" in front of the engineering department building was painted, acting as a type of Blarney Stone for students. Over the years, both Engineers' Rock and Senior Rock have been painted regularly, whether to promote a group or gathering on campus, as a way for students to speak their minds in support of or protest against a current event on or off campus, or just for fun, as seen above in this photograph from 1983.

Former NASA astronaut and local alum José Hernández has visited Pacific many times to give talks and appear at events since his graduation in 1985. Perhaps the most personal event, however, was the 2016 Diploma and Hooding Ceremony of the School of Engineering and Computer Science, at which he hooded his son Julio Hernández.

This photograph shows Engineers' Rock as it was painted for the 2014 Western Regional LGBTQIA College Conference, hosted at Pacific. Among the groups formed at Pacific over the years in support of the LGBTQIA community are the Gay Student Union (created in 1972); the Pacific Gay Alliance (1993), which was quickly renamed the Pacific Gay, Lesbian, Bisexual Alliance; the McGeorge Lambda Law Students Association (1982, on the Sacramento campus); and the Pride Resource Center (2003).

Six

ATHLETICS
SPORTS AND RECREATION

Long before Pacific had actual athletic teams, the sports program started out with just the traditional field day activities, at which various athletic events were arranged for the student body. Some of the first official sports offered at Pacific were tennis, track, bicycle club, football/rugby, baseball, and basketball. Over the years, official teams would come and go according to student interest and what the school's administration would allow. More recently, the continuation of particular teams often came down to monetary considerations, as was the case with football, men's volleyball, and field hockey. Many teams start as intramural or club sports before being recognized as official Pacific teams.

The Women's Athletic Association (WAA) was formed to support women in athletics; its slogan was "A sport for every woman. Every woman in a sport." In the 1950s, the organization was renamed the Women's Recreation Association (WRA). These early organizations laid the foundation for the strong women's athletic programs that currently exist at the university. Another student organization focused on furthering athletic activities and recruitment was the Block P Society, which was started in the early 1920s. Athletes who earned a letter in their sport could gain membership to the society, which was known for participating in charitable endeavors.

Pacific has produced over 160 All-American athletes, beginning in 1943 with Art McCaffray and John Podesto in football. In 1977, Jana Brandenburg, Sandra Johnson, Nancy Norman, and Ann Redig became the first women All-Americans for Pacific as team members for the 800-yard freestyle swimming relay. Seven Pacificans have made it to the Olympic Games, and Jennifer Joines-Tamas, Elaina Oden, and Bradley Schumacher all medaled. Others have made it to the national level either as players or coaches, including Pete Carroll, Tom Flores, Eddie LeBaron, and Michael Olowokandi, to name a few.

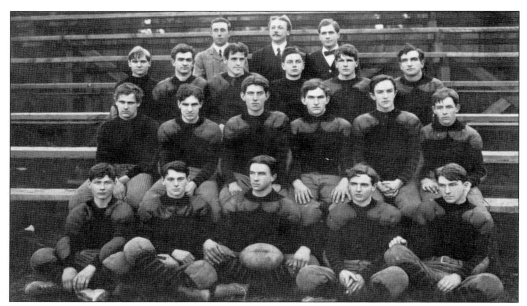

Orange has been Pacific's school color since the very beginning; the first yearbook, published in 1886, was called *Naranjado*, the Spanish word for "orange," and likely references the state flower, the California poppy, which was featured on the 1890 yearbook cover. Over the next several years, various sports teams added black to their uniforms, and looking at these photographs of the 1908 rugby team and 1912 "Foot Ball" team, it is clear why one Pacific publication from that era referred to the design as "tiger stripes." In 1925, the Associated Students Constitution and Bylaws officially designated orange and black as the school colors and confirmed that the official school "emblem" would be a tiger.

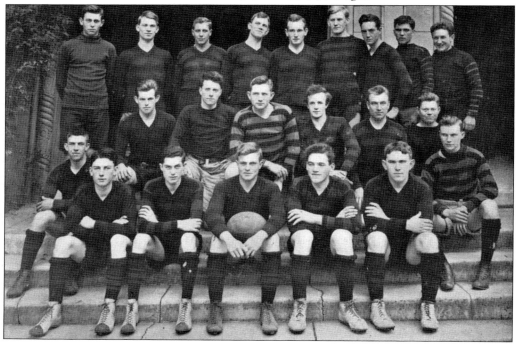

One of the most long-standing women's sports in Pacific's history is basketball. The team is listed in the yearbooks starting in the early 1900s, although interest in and playing of the sport probably started before that time. This photograph from the mid-1920s shows the style of uniform that was worn at the time; previous designs included even more fabric.

Erwin "Swede" Righter coached football at Pacific from 1921 to 1932, but for the 1930–1931 season, he also coached the varsity basketball team, as seen here. Righter himself was an Olympic gold medalist, having played on the US rugby team in the 1920 Summer Games.

Bonfires had been lit at various events during Pacific's history, but it was not until 1926 that the Bonfire Rally became the traditional activity for the night before the homecoming football game. A group of students, usually lower classmen, were assigned to guard the structure until the night of the rally, just in case students from a rival school tried to ignite it early. After 1968, pollution concerns turned the Bonfire Rally into pep rallies, and although there was a brief revival in the 1980s and then a "special ground effects fireworks show and display" in the 1990s, today the Bonfire Rally is a thing of the past.

Pictured is the 1939 season's football team onboard the SS *Lurline* in Pearl Harbor. Pacific beat the University of Hawaii team 19-6 that December. Coach Amos Alonzo Stagg is on the far right. Stagg is the winningest coach at Pacific, with a 60-77-7 record.

The 1949 season football team remains one of Pacific's best. The team was undefeated and ranked 10th in the nation, and yet it was not invited to any bowl games, as commemorated in the slogan "Undefeated, Untied, and Uninvited!" Fifteen of the players went on to the National Football League (NFL) draft, including Eddie Macon, Walter Polenske, Don Hardey, Harry Kane, John Rohde, Bob Moser, Sid Hall, Ken Johnson, Don Campora, Bob Heck, John Poulos, Richard Batten, Patrick Ribeiro, Duane Putman, and All-American Eddie LeBaron. Seventy-three total players from Pacific football history have been drafted into the NFL.

All-American football player Eddie LeBaron (center) graduated from Pacific in 1950. Shortly after the Washington Redskins drafted him, he was called to service as a Marine in the Korean War. He returned to the NFL two years later, after being discharged following an injury in combat. At five feet, seven inches tall, LeBaron is known as one of the smallest quarterbacks to ever play in the NFL. LeBaron is seen here in 1967 with Johnny Rogers (left) at the annual varsity versus alumni football game.

Costume mascots first appeared at Pacific in 1949 with Tommy Tiger and Tillie Tiger (sometimes spelled Tilly). According to the 1952 yearbook, Bev Borror wore the Tillie suit that year, and Jim Williams wore Tommy (left). In the same year, Barbara Baglini and Barbara (Andress) McCarty suited up as Fluffy and Tuffy (right).

Baxter Stadium was the site at which the first American citizen ran the mile in less than four minutes. University of California at Berkeley student Don Bowden completed the mile in three minutes and 58.7 seconds at Pacific on June 1, 1957. Baxter Stadium was razed in 1961 after athletic events were moved to Stagg Stadium and the land was needed for the cluster colleges.

.00 S. CALIF. ST.
PHONE 3-3578

The Victory Bell made its debut in 1949 at the Pacific–San Jose State University (SJSU) football game. The Alpha Kappa Phi (Archania) fraternity commissioned the bell, which has an orange *P* on a black background on one side and a gold *SJ* on a blue background on the other. The Tiger-Spartan rivalry goes back to their first football game in 1921, when the teams were crosstown neighbors prior to Pacific's move to Stockton. Over the years, the bell moved back and forth with the winner (Pacific won it in 1949), and the tradition continued until their final game in 1995, when Pacific's team was disbanded for financial reasons. Pacific won that game 32-30, but the bell remained in San Jose. For a time, the tradition was carried on between the Tiger and Spartan basketball teams, the last being in 2009. Since 2018, the Victory Bell has been on loan from SJSU to the 49ers Museum at Levi's Stadium, where it is part of an exhibit on Bay Area college football.

Sometime after the mid-1950s, Tillie Tiger disappeared, but then in the 1959 yearbook there is mention of Tessie the Tiger. The following year, Tammy the Tiger appeared alongside Tommy. It is unknown whether the name Tillie was forgotten on accident or rebranded on purpose. Tommy and Tammy, like Tommy and Tillie, were regular sights at rallies (above) and games (below) for several years, but by the mid-1960s, the female mascot disappeared, and by 1976, Tommy was gone as well.

Pacific had the same school colors and mascot as Princeton University, and some claimed the duplication was intentional, although there is no evidence to support the contention. Many schools had the same mascot in the early days, and in fact at one time the tiger was ranked the second-most popular collegiate mascot. Pacific's tiger has undergone many transformations since its first appearance in 1949. In some cases, it was barely recognizable as a tiger, but it has nonetheless always imbued the fierce spirit of Pacific.

Tom Flores came to Pacific in 1956 on an academic scholarship, and he earned a bachelor's degree and a teaching credential in 1959. Flores was almost done completing his master's degree, which he was working on while coaching Pacific's football team, but he left in 1960 to join the American Football League's Oakland Raiders as a quarterback. He went on to play for several other teams and then transitioned into a coaching career. He married Pacifican Barbara Fridell in 1961. According to the *Pacific Review*, Flores was "one of only two people in history to win a Super Bowl as a player (Chiefs), assistant coach (Raiders), and head coach (Raiders)." Flores was also the first Mexican American starting quarterback and the first minority head coach in professional football history to win a Super Bowl.

The rally commission often booked special guests to show up to pregame events. One memorable visitor was singer and actor Sammy Davis Jr., who sang and did impersonations during a 1958 Friday night rally and then returned on Saturday for the football game, at which he led the Pacific Rooters pep squad in the clap yell. Pictured are, from left to right, (first row) Denny Levett, Sharon Kenney, and Janet Barron; (second row) Rich Roberts, Micky Babb, Sammy Davis Jr., Tommy Tiger, Donna Hudson, and Rick Gilbert.

Pictured is the 1959 Pacific football team arriving in Hawaii, where it would beat the University of Hawaii team 6-0. Jack "Moose" Myers, who coached the team from 1953 to 1960, guided Pacific in five straight winning seasons, and 20 of his players went on to be selected in the NFL draft.

The Hub Theater, on Market Street in San Francisco, was known as the "The Little Theatre with the Big Marquee" and was supposedly owned for a time by a Pacific alum. During the late 1950s and early 1960s, when Pacific's basketball team played in San Francisco, the owner would put up the score and a message on the marquee.

Pacific baseball coach Tom Stubbs is shown accepting the first-place trophy for the Marines' Easter Baseball Tournament on April 15, 1965. Also pictured are Maj. Gen. Bruno A. Hochmuth (far left) and Maj. R.E. Downen (far right). Pacific beat San Francisco State 12-0 for the championship. Stubbs coached at Pacific from 1964 to 1971 and then again from 1973 to 1981, earning a 410-384 record that included the 1968 season, when the team broke 27 school records and tied another 5.

Scott Boras was captain of the baseball team until he earned his pharmacy degree in 1977 and went on to play minor-league baseball. He later returned to Pacific and earned his law degree in 1982. Boras then became a sports agent, specializing in baseball, and is the founder, owner, and president of the Boras Corporation. Some of the athletes he negotiated for were Bill Caudill and Keith Hernandez. *Forbes* has repeatedly named Boras the "Most Powerful Sports Agent" in the world.

PETE CARROLL

NFL football coach and Vince Lombardi Trophy winner Pete Carroll transferred in on a scholarship in the fall of 1971 and played two seasons as a Pacific Tiger. Carroll earned his bachelor's degree in 1973, his master's in 1978, and then returned for his teaching credentials, all at Pacific. According to the *Pacific Review*, "He also met his wife, Pacific volleyball player Glena (Goranson) '77, on campus when he was a graduate assistant. An accomplished athlete in her own right, she was Pacific's first female scholarship athlete."

Benny Buggs (with trophy) and Terence Carney (with net) celebrate their PCAA Tournament victory against Utah State. By winning the Pacific Coast Athletic Association tournament, Pacific's 1978 basketball team moved on to the National Collegiate Athletic Association (NCAA) playoffs. The next spring, in his last season as coach at Pacific, Stan Morrison received PCAA and Northern California Coach of the Year honors.

The Tommy Tiger mascot costume was lost or stolen in 1976, and Pacific did not have a costumed mascot again until 1981, when Bill McCarty revitalized the position with the creation of Super Tiger. McCarty was inspired by the stories he had heard from his mother, Barbara (Andress) McCarty, who had been a mascot at Pacific 30 years prior.

The first national sports title in Pacific's history was won by the women's volleyball team in 1985 after it beat Stanford at the NCAA tournament. It won the NCAA Division I Volleyball National Championship a second time the following year against Nebraska at home. All-American Elaina Oden went on to play at the 1992 Summer Olympic Games, where the US volleyball team won the bronze medal. At the Spanos Center in 1986 are, from left to right, Brooke Herrington, Dorothy Hert, Elizabeth Hert, Teri McGrath, Mary Miller, and Elaina Oden.

University of the Pacific • Weekly news since 1908 • Volume 86 • Issue 14 • February 8, 1996

UOP says goodbye to 77 years of football tradition

DAVID OTTENFELD
Pacifican Staff Writer

UOP's decision to suspend its rich football tradition left the school's athletic future in doubt and prompted reactions ranging from regret to remorse.

"The Board of Regents strongly supports the total athletic program, but with great reluctance we agreed to suspend football on a temporary basis," Board of Regents Chairman Robert Monagan said after the Regents voted December 19 to end the 77 year old program.

The debate over football has raged for more than 40 years on campus. In the end, the key factor, as always, was finance.

"I think that it's a real loss for the university, and therefore it's going to leave a hole in the university. We're going to feel it in the fall," President Donald DeRosa said in an interview.

"At the same time, of course, I know that the board was looking at the balance sheet, and this year we were looking at a $400,000 loss. Next year, because of the complica-

letic Director Bob Lee.

The regents made their decision after examining the pros and cons of keeping football. In the 1994-95 season, football ended the fiscal year $800,000 in the red, not including the program's 82 athletic scholarships, DeRosa said in a written statement.

"If somebody tells you that you have cancer, and you have to have something removed, you're not happy about it, but you're relieved you made the right decision. In this particular case it appears that we've made the right decision for the entire university," said Regent Gary Podesto.

For more on Football see page 7, 8, 20

Regent James McCargo agreed. "I'll miss football very much, and I'm sad it had to be done," McCargo said. "But on the other hand, as board members, our job is to make the decisions that will make the school more viable in the future."

The decision was made before the spring semester to help football play-

Amos Alonzo Stagg Stadium sits empty after the Board of Regents' December decision to suspend the football program. For student speculation into future uses for the facility, see Opinion, p. 7.

Canine determines arson cause of dining hall fire

In December 1995, the board of regents voted to suspend the football program. Football had been at Pacific for 77 years, but due to financial instability, the program was no longer feasible. This was not the first time football had been brought to the chopping block; President Burns had also dealt with the issue 40 years prior.

All-American senior Brad Schumacher won two Olympic gold medals at the 1996 Summer Games in Atlanta. The first medal was as part of the 800-meter freestyle relay team, and the second was for the 400-meter relay. Schumacher went on to graduate from Pacific the following spring and then returned to receive his master's in business administration in 2005.

All-American and number-one overall National Basketball Association (NBA) draft pick Michael Olowokandi graduated from Pacific in 1998. Olowokandi led Pacific to its first Big West Conference Championship in 1997. In a quote from the *Pacific Review*, he shares his thoughts on what his parents felt about the draft pick: "I think they were proudest of me that day in Stockton when I got my degree."

The final and most current rendition of the tiger mascot is Powercat. The mascot underwent a makeover in 1998, and Tommy was retired. The new mascot and logo were created to further the goal of having Pacific's teams be "identified in a strong, powerful way," according to the *Pacific Review*.

Rugby is one of the sports that has come and gone and come again over the course of the school's history. In 2015, Pacific's rugby club won the National Small College Rugby Organization Challenge Cup—its first national title since the team appeared on campus in the early 1900s.

DISCOVER THOUSANDS OF LOCAL HISTORY BOOKS FEATURING MILLIONS OF VINTAGE IMAGES

Arcadia Publishing, the leading local history publisher in the United States, is committed to making history accessible and meaningful through publishing books that celebrate and preserve the heritage of America's people and places.

Find more books like this at
www.arcadiapublishing.com

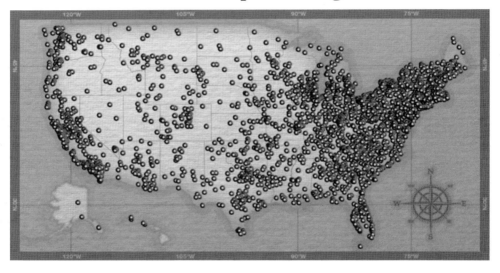

Search for your hometown history, your old stomping grounds, and even your favorite sports team.